PRAISE FOR

Common sense book f̶ ...̶.̶.̶.̶.̶.̶.̶.̶a̶n̶ teens!
— *Library Journal*

WHAT A GREAT RESOURCE! Robin Henry's voice is one that young Black people NEED to hear. It still astounds me that so many young Black people, so many young people in general, even those that have made it as far as the college classroom, still need the polish and professionalism that Robin so expertly details in her book. I will most certainly read this text with my students, and with my own children.
   —Detmer Wells, Instructor, Governors State University

We need more straight talk, dedication, and attention to detail like Robin's. She really speaks her truth with extreme clarity in "No Mistakes"; to the point that I can make no mistake about her position. **I PARTICULARLY LIKE ROBIN'S PRACTICAL TIPS TO TEENS ON IMAGE AND VARIOUS USEFUL FORMS OF WRITTEN AND VERBAL COMMUNICATION.** She shows that it's about paying attention to what you are saying to people—it's all language, verbal and non-verbal. Coming from her, a former English teacher, so so appropriate. Her advice proves effective with the former student and gang leader who says that youth should strive to be leaders, not followers; that they must give and receive respect. Robin's leadership by example in "No Mistakes" commands my respect.
   —Deborah Barnett-Smith, Marketing Consultant

KUDOS TO ROBIN FOR TELLING TEENS THE TRUTH! Remember the Emperor's New Clothes tale...we all see it but no one wants to say it. Luckily Robin took the lead...the rest of the village thanks you for helping out.
   —Karen M. Wilcher, Table Matters

HY

Robin Henry's book, "No Mistakes", **is timely, appropriate and well thought out** book that is a great source of advice and information for today's youth. Today, African-American youths have so many obstacles, distractions and detractors working against them, that resources on how to carry themselves, what is appropriate and how to function in today's collegiate and business setting is long overdue. I mentor students in the Memphis area, and many times there really aren't resources or books that we can refer students to; many times it's hard to tell young people what you really want to tell them without feelings being hurt. This is a great book and one that I know will be well received.

    —Jeff Robbins, Marketing Project Manager
      FedEx Corporate Services

I have known Robin all my life, she is a straight shooter…**This is a message that our youth need to hear!** I mentor African American adolescents in my community regularly and can tell you wholeheartedly, that our children need this book and the guidance within. Unfortunately, so many lack positive role models to give them these important life lessons, and in turn they fall through the cracks and become statistics. We must use every tool at our disposal to prevent this from happening for the future of our children's children.

    —CPT Andre A. Batiste, Sr., B Co, USAG Commanding

This is *a wonderful book for African-Amercian teenagers* written in a language that they understand. I look forward to sharing it with my patients.

    —Angela H. Mahome, M.D., Child and Adolescent
      Psychiatrist

NO MISTAKES:

The African American Teen Guide to Growing Up Strong

By Robin Henry

NO MISTAKES:

The African American Teen Guide to Growing Up Strong

By Robin Henry

Amber Books

Phoenix

New York   Los Angeles

NO MISTAKES:
The African American Teen Guide to Growing Up Strong

by Robin Henry

Published by:
Amber Books
A Division of Amber Communications Group, Inc.
1334 East Chandler Boulevard, Suite 5-D67
Phoenix, AZ 85048
amberbk@aol.com
WWW.AMBERBOOKS.COM

Tony Rose, Publisher/Editorial Director   Samuel P. Peabody, Associate Publisher
Yvonne Rose, Associate Publisher/Sr Editor   Jannie M. Lathan, Associate Publisher
The Printed Page, Interior & Cover Design

Library of Congress
Catalog-in-Publication Information Pending
2005

Acknowledgments

My mom, Jane Williams, taught me most of the information in this guidebook. My family has issues and high standards regarding image, communications and etiquette. My son Grayson Brooks, my nephew Brian Todd and my niece Jamie Lauren helped me with copies, emails, folders, and insight. My sister, Karen and her husband, Brian gave me advice. My husband George looked over my work and helped me along the way. I learned a lot and made plenty of mistakes while on the job!

Very special thanks to some extraordinary people:

▼ George F. Henry, Jr., LCSW—**Support & Love**

▼ Nannette Howard & Mary Howard-Chitty—**Makeup lessons**

▼ Martha, Bambi, Sarah, Sole—**Beauty experts**

▼ Karen Johnson—**Workouts and encouragement**

▼ Karen Mitchell-Wilcher—**Etiquette updates**

▼ Ruth Martin and Lorraine Simpson—**Image advisors**

▼ Jeff Robbins and Andrea Knowles—**Travel guides**

▼ Michelle Garner, Jeff Cullers, Charles Mingo, Diane L. Jackson—**Guidance**

▼ Shatese, Chanel, Monique, Tanekkia, Nicci—**Youthful inspiration**

▼ Dee Daniels, Elroy Reed, Pluria Marshall ….and My Publisher Tony Rose—**Making my dreams become a reality**

You all really taught me well…

- ▼ The Professional Woman Network

- ▼ My sorors of Alpha Kappa Alpha Sorority, Inc.

- ▼ My friends: Lorraine Graves-Simpson, Darlene Foster-DeJohnette, Karen Collymore-Johnson, Brian Johnson, Karen Mitchell-Wilcher, Michelle White-Martin, Karen Coleman, Susan Hearn, Gina Hemphill, Debbie Edwards, Angela Hicks-Skinner, Janis Robinson, Pluria Marshall Jr., Lerone Bennett III, Terry Calloway, Donald Johnson, Steve McKeever, Michael Hughes, Tony Resendez, Steven Berry & Marvin Whaley

Finally, I did not invent the advice presented here, I just wrote down what works. I reviewed newspaper columns, read magazine columns, surfed the Internet for web sites of a variety of companies just to be sure that others agree with my advice!

All I really did was package the information so that you have a quick guide when you need it the most.

Words to remember:

> *Classic style endures time and appeals to those who count!*
> *Always do your best to be your best!*

About the Author, Robin Henry

Robin Henry grew up in Chicago and its south suburbs and still calls this area home. She earned her B.A. in Rhetoric/Speech Communications from the University of Illinois at Urbana-Champaign and her M.A.T. in Teaching Secondary English from Columbia College Chicago. Robin is the Curriculum Coordinator at Englewood Tech Prep Academy, one of the Chicago Public Schools. Her responsibilities include participation on the Student Development Program, Small Schools Committee, Literacy and Administrative Advisory Teams.

Most recently, Robin served as the English Department Chairman. She has been an urban teacher in the inner city since 1994 when she began teaching at DuSable High School. She has taught World, American, and Survey of Literature; Creative Writing; and Speech Communications. The author is the proud mother of one son, Grayson and she is married to George Henry, Jr. Robin is a member of Alpha Kappa Alpha Sorority, Inc. and the National Association of African American Journalists.

Who's Who Among America's Teachers has selected Robin Mitchell-Henry for inclusion in the 2005 list of outstanding educators.

No Mistakes

Contents

Acknowledgments vii
About the Author, Robin Henry ix

Get it together! Present a POWERful Image 1
What difference does your image make? 2
You are your Image! Think about it 4
Sometimes…Hair is Everything! 5
All Hair is…Good Hair… 7
She just did not know… 10
Makeup…Wear it well 12
Nails send Messages 13
Just… a Hint of Fragrance 13
What to wear? Wardrobe begins with WAR… 14
That well-scrubbed look… 16
Looking Cheap Will Cost You… 18
Don't even go there! 19
Clean up your act! 20
Fitness…Get with a plan! 21

Say What? Communication Counts 25
Communication Is Much More Than Just Words! 26
Can you hear me now? 27
Make them hear your speech! 28
Your REPUTATION—It's all about YOU… 29
Communication issues to think about… 30
First Impressions Last Forever! 31
Learn some new words! 33
He said, she said… 34

Where is Your Home-training? Etiquette Matters. . . 37
Eating Out?…Make A Good Impression 38
Traveling? Quick Tips for an Enjoyable Trip… 40
Rival Schools Meet. 41
Staying in touch the right way… 42
Where Are Your Manners? …Test Your Knowledge Now… . . . 43
Fit in or get out 44
Know the GAME! 46

Going to College? Apply For All Scholarships! 49

Do your best to get a scholarship! 50
The A-Student Who Did Not Know How to Study 51
Planning your College Schedule 53
Study Guidelines 54
Some Students Have it ALL 56
Look EVERYWHERE for scholarships! 58
Vital Words: Be a Professional *60*

The Right Stuff Resumes, Cover Letters, Job Applications. 63

What do they want? *64*
Follow these hints to write a great resume... 65
Resumes Do Matter!!—Sometimes Being Too Cool Is Not Cool
   At All **66**
Fill in the blanks for a rough draft of your own resume 68
Examples of Work Experience... 70
Cover Letters 72
The Job Application 74

Lights, Camera, Action Pull It All Together For Your Interview 77

Interview Questions 78
Looking for a job? Going to college? Need a scholarship? 79
Successful Interviews—Putting it all together, preparation,
   looks, effort 80
The real deal: The interview, the meeting, the speech... 82
What is a network?. 83
Want a job...Get ready to work! 85
Get a job, any job! 86

About the Author—Fact Sheet 91

Introduction

Before you even get started, I want you to know that **this book was written for you**. Teenagers just like you inspired me because of what they wanted to know, but did not already know. **Check it out,** you may learn something!

You want to act grown? Think about what you do, before you do it. There are too many **African American teens** out there **making mistakes** by using **drugs**, having **sex**…babies making **babies**…and going to **prison**. You know them, ask one and **they will tell you** not to make the same mistakes that they did.

As an **African American mother**, I am tired of so much bad news and I am not having it for my son. As an **African American teacher**, I know I can reach out to **you** and **your friends.**

I was **not born rich or royal**, so I have to work for a living. I am not famous like a rap artist or a star in the **WNBA**, so I had to find another way to make money. Soon you will have to figure out how to **get paid.** Check out this book and try to learn something about yourself, then use it!

That's right, teachers are always telling you to read another book, right? This is different. My students, **African-American teens from the 'hood**, asked me to put this valuable information in writing so they could use it now and later. Please believe—there are no jokes in the real world. Everybody is trying to make it and some folks are struggling just to survive.

There is **nothing wrong** with you or the way you are doing things. Just know that **we can all improve**. We can all **learn to be better.** After working with teens and listening to their issues, I have learned quite a bit. I suggest that you open this book and **pay attention**. Why? Why not? You think that you can have anything you want just because you say so? Wrong answer! **Get it straight;** you will have to compete with many others for a grade, a chance to go to college, trade school or the military. Then, you will have to be **better than everyone else** just to get some attention and a get good job. Sometimes we need others for the answers when we are confused.

I asked a **gang leader** to help me to understand how to keep my students out of **trouble.** He said, "Teach them to be leaders, not just followers and above all, they should give and expect respect." Readers—now you will have to **decide what to do…**

—**Robin Henry**
June 2005

Get it together!
Present a POWERful Image

What difference does your image make?

▼ You need to **get paid!** Soon you will try to get a job for **the first time.** Competition for every job is fierce. Companies are very careful about hiring the right person. They will **trash your application** for something very small. Never let a sloppy image mess you up. Show them you can handle their business because you can **handle *your own* business!**

▼ After that, you may want to start a career! Recent college graduates are looking for *entry-level* career opportunities. You have to face the fact that others may have experience and education. You need to look willing but not desperate, and pulled together, but not stuffy.

▼ After working for a year, you are going to want a promotion! Then you will have to stand out to get noticed. By then you have made many impressions on your boss—some good and some bad. Your actions, your work, AND your image must work together to give decision-makers more confidence in you!

▼ One day you may want to reach out and get more. If you want to have more money, you will have to build up your business. Everyone wants the same thing that you want. So you need better clothes, a few new accessories, more expensive shoes, or a tough, new suit.

▼ Look at all your options. *When one person gets a job,* someone else did not get that job. Be on the right side of that decision. Your image is a big deal! Remember the first step: get their attention! Looking good will help get you in the door.

▼ Even if you never had a job, one day you will have one. Your job search will be challenging, but not impossible. This is the perfect time to improve your image and make it work for you. You must work to impress others with your skills and your potential for success. You need every advantage.

▼ You want to join a club. Persons hoping to join an organization need to influence others to gain acceptance. If you are in certain groups, your opportunities expand into options. Get to know the right groups of people so they can help you to help yourself. The first step is to get in, then make others want to be associated with you!

▼ You need recognition or publicity. If you look good, it brings attention to you. Press is not easy to get. Agents and public relations pros work hard to get stories published for rap stars, athletes, actors, and singers. Your only guarantee is your image. You can get what you want by choosing the right look for every occasion.

Be very SLICK

Style

Looks

Intelligence

Charm

Knowledge

You are your Image! Think about it...

▼ Who cares about image anyway?

▼ Why can't you do whatever with your own hair, nails, clothes, and makeup?

▼ Who is a good role model?

▼ What difference does a good image make?

▼ You want to improve your image? Now what?

▼ What's up with that hair?

▼ Do you get the right kind of attention?

▼ Has anyone told you that your hair looks great lately?

Sometimes...Hair is Everything!

When she first started high school as a freshman, Rianna looked OK, just OK. Her hair was stiff, broken off, and not very healthy. As the years passed she tried every hair trend: braids, extensions, weave, blond highlights, burgundy color, beads, ponytails, French rolls, and teeny-weeny curls.

By the time she was a senior, she asked for some advice. I told her to get a blunt cut bob just below her chin to look stylish and conservative, but still attractive. At first she could not believe how great her hair looked and how good it felt. Without all of the goop and gunk she used before, her hair moved whenever she shook it. She really enjoyed this new style.

I explained that healthy hair should move, and look touchable. I shared a secret: people judge others by looking at them from head to toe, but it all begins with the hair. Hair signifies confidence, attention to detail, and a healthy lifestyle.

> *When your hair looks good, then you look great! Know the difference between over-the-top party hairdos and conservative hairstyles.*

That year, Rianna competed and beat every single senior in the whole city for a full ride UNCF scholarship. The interviewers asked her about the most important lesson she learned from a teacher. She said, "Mrs. Henry told us to polish our image and others would treat us with respect because we'd look like we could handle anything!" They smiled and they told her that was a great lesson, and it was more important that she paid attention and actually followed the advice.

Later that year, she went to Washington, DC to begin her freshman year at Howard University, where some of the most attractive, sophisticated, confident, successful and intimidating young ladies attend school. Because her hair looked so great, she fit right in with the other young ladies who already knew rule #1:

▼ When it comes to a professional image, looks really count and hair is everything!

Recently, she came home for a visit. Her hair is thicker, longer and healthier than ever…she told me that she is still using my advice!

All Hair is…Good Hair…

If you **have hair on your head, it is good hair!** There **is no such thing** as bad hair. Run and **tell that!**

Hair is everything, make no mistake about that! Just be sure your hair is clean, freshly cut and styled in a conservative manner. The ends should be cut every 6 weeks to stay neat and healthy. Out of control hair makes you look out of control. Great hair works for you at school, at work, at parties…

▼ The prom is about the only time that teens need fancy up-do's. Razor-cut symbols carved into the hair are played out. While individual taste matters, chill out with bizarre, hairstyles so that you will fit in at an office, or at church, not just on the dance floor at the local club. Braided styles should be simple and neat. Step away from cheap fake-looking hair weaves, glitter, unnatural colors, yarn, sprinkles, and those nasty, dirty, scrunchies—if you want to look your best!

▼ Girls, your hairstyle should make you look your best and allow you to fit into most situations. Adults respect teens with hair that looks clean and healthy. Make an effort to look your best, but don't play yourself. Looking too good can attract the wrong type of attention too! It looks flirty to play with your hair or blow it out of your face. Choose a style that allows you to appear confident and in control without much fuss.

▼ Your hair should help you to look your age. If you wear hair accessories such as headbands and ponytail holders, you may look younger. Get to know your own head of hair. Everyone cannot have the same hairstyle, so choose one that works without lots of effort. Do you have thick, thin, or medium hair? The texture of your hair can make or break your style.

▼ Curly, nappy, or kinky? Don't even try a bone-straight style because it makes no sense. It will easily revert with a small amount of exposure to humidity.

▼ If your hair grows slowly, is very thin, or extremely unhealthy, opt for a short cut. You will accomplish two things at the same time. A good shorter cut will give you a "pulled together" appearance. You will have a chance to improve the health of your hair and give it a time to grow gracefully.

▼ Long hair or long, thin split ends? If you want long hair, it only looks good if it is thick and healthy. It takes time to care for your hair; you just need to know what to do.

▼ Get a good blunt cut and trim every 6-8 weeks. Wash and condition once a week. Wet set hair on hard magnetic rollers and sit under a dryer. Do not use blow dryers, hot curlers, flat irons, and gel. Sleep on silk pillowcases. Do not pull hair too tightly. When hair gets dry, wash and condition it. Forget grease, it looks awful and rarely helps your hair. Talk to a licensed hair stylist, not your friend who knows how to whip her hair!

▼ Guys do not slap big globs of grease in your hair. Most grown men with successful careers do not wear braided styles. So go for a clean-cut look. Growing up means looking like you mean business.

▼ Short hair, freshly cut hair always looks neat with business attire. Perhaps you are old enough to have a clean-cut style that you see in the pages of Ebony, Jet, or African American Enterprise, not Right On.

▼ Hair should be cut close enough to make your head look appealing, but not appalling. Every style is not for every head. Think about the shape of your head. If you have fat rolls in the back of your head, then do not wear your hair cut real short. You need to look like you have some business, not like your barber laughed as you walked away.

▼ Know that growing up means it may be time to lose the multi-colored strands, long braids, beads, pony tails, afro puffs, cut-in designs, and long locks that are so popular. Sometimes change is good in the long run.

She just did not know...

As I sat in my classroom one day, Treena knocked at the door and asked to come in for a few minutes. She looked serious and rather troubled, so I stopped grading papers to give her my full attention.

Her problem was unusual since I never had the same experience and I was rather shocked when she finished her story. The previous day, Treena went downtown for a job interview. She told me that she saw an advertisement in the newspaper. She called the number and scheduled an appointment for an interview. They told her to bring a resume and come dressed to impress.

Treena said that she went shopping for the right outfit: new boots, jeans, a matching plaid purse, belt and cap, a denim blouse, and a zodiac ring-necklace-earrings set. She spent $200 on her outfit because she wanted to look perfect. She told me that she had her hair dyed bright burgundy and she wore her burgundy shades, burgundy eye shadow, and burgundy lip-gloss. She thought she was a dime, a perfect 10 as she walked into the office for the interview.

You know you judge other people! Don't like to admit it, but I do it too. People admit they make snap judgments in 30 seconds based only on someone's looks. Sometimes the people making those judgments can hire or fire you, pass or fail you, or even make a life-changing decision about you.

When she handed the receptionist her resume, and asked for an application, but she was denied. The receptionist told her that she was not properly attired for a job interview and she should leave immediately. As Treena turned around, she noticed the other girls in the lobby. They were all wearing dark suits, low-heeled pumps, small earrings, and they carried leather briefcases. They looked all old and stale, but they were all waiting for the chance to get a job. A chance that Treena no longer had.

I explained to her that casual clothes and interview suits were two different things. In order to stand out in an interview, you need to wear the right "uniform" so that the interviewer will pay attention to you—not get all caught up in your clothes.

Makeup... Wear it well

Less is more! You should look like you are ready to deal with anything. Grown women look immature and incomplete without makeup. But too much on teenagers is just wrong! Go to a department store and visit the makeup counter. They will help you.

Most teens can use a little bit of mascara and lip-gloss and look ready to go! For important occasions, a bit of blush adds warmth to your cheeks. If you have problems with acne, see your doctor for a skin-care treatment.

Nails send Messages

Nails send messages so make sure you send the right message. Manicured and attractive nails show others that you know small things count.

Ladies

▼ Size of nail should be on the short side, no longer than ¼ inch from fingertips. The shape should be square-oval. If you use polish, the color should be neutral with a matte finish, not frosted, and no glitter. Just say no to long, fake, tips and the designed and studded nails.

Fellas

▼ Keep nails very short, very neat, and very clean.

▼ No clear polish…enough said!

Just… a Hint of Fragrance

Don't let them smell you before you get inside the door. Spray one spritz of cologne into the air, above your head. Walk under the spray, and you will have all you will need.

What to wear? Wardrobe begins with WAR...

Rules to remember to be ready for ANYTHING:

- ▼ Outfits should be sharp—not sexy

- ▼ Don't know for sure? You'd better ask somebody!

- ▼ With jewelry—less is more

- ▼ Small earrings for ladies, no earring for fellas—you heard that?

- ▼ Polished shoes—always

- ▼ Wear a suit, yes, a SUIT

Wardrobe Checklist
Business

For Young Women
Dark suit w/pants & skirt
White blouses
Neutral & Black stockings
2" inch pumps
Dark trousers
Dark twin sweater set
Trench coat
Good bras

For Young Men
Dark single breasted suit
Starched white shirts
Dark socks
Wing tips, tie ups & loafers
Thin high quality cotton T-shirts
Dark sports coat
Ties w/small repeat patterns, stripes
Trench coat w/lining

Casual

For Girls
Khakis
Polo shirt
Twin set
Loafers
Big Black sunglasses

For Guys
Khakis
Polo shirt
v-neck sweater
loafers
Wire rimmed sunglasses

Formal

For Ladies
Gown
Gold or silver watch
Earrings
High heels
Small purse

For Gents
Tuxedo
Gold or silver watch
Cuff links
Dark shoes
Handkerchief

Active

For everybody
Cross trainers / sandals / loafers   Polo shir
Long shorts   Tennis outfit
Swimming attire & /Sunglasses & Windbreaker
White socks

That well-scrubbed look...

When you want to get something important like a job, there are rules to follow!

Clothing

The right fit fits right in! Fitting in is better than standing out. Think about it, do you have any business? Yes? Strut your stuff properly. Business people are not cool or hip and they don't want to see you that way. Save your fly gear for another time.

You'd better recognize who you are. Work with what you've got. Believe in yourself. Learn to like yourself and the features, complexion, and body you were born with! Show off the good stuff, cover up the flaws.

Right now you need quality clothes that are comfortable and basic, not trendy. Use your clothes to give you that pulled together look. Make them trust you. Don't get caught up in uncomfortable clothes that make you twitch and scratch. Make your clothes work with you.

Shoes

Many managers check out your shoes if they want to check you out. Be comfortable, but come correct. Don't wear high heels to a job interview. This will get the wrong type of attention! Guys should match your belt and socks to your shoes. Clean your shoes then use some polish.

Jewelry

Don't mess up everything with loud jewelry. Less is always more. Ladies can wear one pair of small earrings and necklaces. Guys should leave your earrings at home! Wear a simple watch with a leather strap for the office and gold or silver for evening. Don't forget that everyone is watching you at all times.

Engaged or married? You should always wear those rings, but that is it. Don't wear bangles, charm bracelets, and diamond/rhinestones jewelry into an office.

Looking Cheap Will Cost You...

Every year at every high school, the senior class plans the Prom. They look forward to the event and everything that goes with it. The girls shop, search, select, get fitted, and finally wear the most elegant dress they can imagine…elegance is in the eye of the beholder.

You see, one young lady named, Samyra, tried to be different. She just wanted to have her own style for one night, a style that was different than what her mom thought was elegant. As I recall, Samyra's family was strict and very religious. They went to church several times each week. The prom dress that Samyra wanted to wear was skin-tight, gold metallic material with a slit up each side. Her shoes were high-heels with straps that wrapped up her leg.

> *People are always going to judge you by the way you look. Know this because looks really do count. I am not talking about becoming a cookie-cutter or Xerox version of your friends. Don't try to stand out for the wrong reasons. Get a grip and know when to be trendy and stylish, and also when to be buttoned up.*

Samyra's mom had a fit and tore up the dress the week before the prom when Samyra brought it home from the store. Samyra cried, screamed and begged, but her mom said, "No daughter of mine will be seen looking like a hooker!" Samyra was grounded and did not go to the Prom, all because she forgot that looking like a lady will never hurt anyone, but looking like a hooker can cost you more than you know.

Don't even go there!

This stuff is all messed up:
- ▼ Processed hair: too curly, too straight, too greasy, too blond, too dark, too many highlights
- ▼ Tight clothes
- ▼ Too much bling-bling
- ▼ Street slang, profanity
- ▼ Bad manners
- ▼ Long nails with designs
- ▼ Visible body piercings, tattoos, or body hair
- ▼ Bright colored shoes, socks, stockings, or jewelry
- ▼ Super thin eyebrows

Scents should make sense, work it right!
- ▼ Too much cologne—less is more
- ▼ body odors—remember to bathe, shower, use deodorant, repeat daily
- ▼ dirty hair—shampoo & condition once a week
- ▼ smelly feet—wash, use lotion, add foot deodorant if needed
- ▼ bad breath—brush and floss at least twice a day
- ▼ any hint of alcohol—don't drink PERIOD
- ▼ chewing gum—use to freshen breath, but chew with mouth shut
- ▼ cigars, cigarettes, smoke of any type—don't smoke PERIOD

Take pride in yourself; don't be dirty because that is nasty

- ▼ Take a bath

- ▼ Spend time with soap and water

- ▼ Wash and iron your clothes

- ▼ Scrub your nails

- ▼ Blow your nose

Clean up your act!

- ▼ Check your hygiene

- ▼ Make sure you smell great, not too sweet or strong

- ▼ Take a long, hard look in the mirror

- ▼ Choose the right clothes, if you don't know, ask somebody

- ▼ Say it right, don't try too hard, just be polite

- ▼ Make your move at the right time

- ▼ Be smooth and smile

When do you have to do this?

- ▼ Talking with grown folks like teachers, pastors, managers, coaches, doctors, customers, clients, and managers

- ▼ To get a better grade while doing a speech

- ▼ Meeting someone older

- ▼ Working at your job

- ▼ Checking out someone to date

- ▼ Going out to a special occasion like the Prom

- ▼ During an interview for a job, scholarship, college, sorority/ fraternity, or internship

Fitness...Get with a plan!

Fit or just fat? You aren't fooling anybody, not even yourself. Do you have to squeeze into your jeans? Can other people see your rolls through your clothes? Can you run 1 lap around the track without stopping?

Quit eating up everything and push away from the table. Too many hot fries for breakfast, onion rings, French fries, chocolate shakes, gyros, chicken wings, and Sub sandwiches for lunch, full meals for late-night snacks, with no exercise just means you are FAT! No disrespect, but being fat is not healthy. Get it together and get in shape. You will look better, feel better and others will respect you quicker.

Why even try? You will:
- ▼ Do your work faster
- ▼ Won't be sick all of the time
- ▼ Have more energy to do other things
- ▼ Be a role-model for your friends
- ▼ Live longer
- ▼ More attractive to the fellas or the ladies...

Being fat is not healthy. People in our culture like great bodies. Just look at the TV and in the magazines. They are crazy and everyone is always on a diet or trying some new workout plan. So don't go to extremes, but you are young, so be healthy, don't wait till you are too old to do anything.

> *Looking good makes others think highly of you. You can control what they see and maybe what they think of you. Represent yourself the right way!*

Once you get in shape, you have to keep that body. Find something that you enjoy and make it a habit. Take some time to exercise. Make it fun, do it with somebody else. Just do it every single day! You can burn calories and fat by walking, biking, dancing, running, aerobics, skating, and kickboxing. Be determined to make a positive change!

Exercise, eat right, drink 8 glasses of water, get 8 hours of sleep, go to church, and love somebody!

Get the 411 on Image

▼ Play up your best features! Always try to look your best. Forget trends, fit should flatter. Please, please, please cover up your problems

▼ Don't look like a lame! Nobody wants to look at your flaws. Show off your shape, not your skin.

▼ Dress to impress! Have clothes for business, casual, formal, & sports

▼ Get ready to wear many hats. Look your best always!

▼ Update and upgrade clothes and accessories. Forget about fashion and trendy gear—wear classics for true style.

▼ Be chic on a budget. Shop around before you buy anything. Make your money stretch. Check out sales, outlets, coupons, and price adjustments.

Say What?
Communication Counts

Communication Is Much More Than Just Words!

Body Language (attitude, look, action)

▼ Open up and be friendly

▼ Believe in yourself

▼ Never let them see you sweat

▼ Trust somebody, but not everybody

▼ Outshine your competition.

▼ Wear the right stuff

▼ Say it, but say it right

Non-Verbal skills

▼ Look people in the eye, don't look down

▼ Stand tall, hands behind your back

▼ Give people some space

(Actions) Before you speak...

▼ Want to fit in; they pay attention to how things are done.

▼ Pause and think for a moment before you answer questions.

▼ Watch your tone and volume, don't scream at people

▼ Not too fast or too slow.

▼ Somewhere in between loud and soft is just right.

Keep your hands to yourself (Mannerisms)

▼ Control yourself

▼ Watch what you do with your hands

▼ Cool out!

Can you hear me now?

Communication does count

▼ Your *barber and hairstylist would leave you all jacked up if they didn't listen! Think about it!*

▼ Learn some new words.

▼ Say it the right way! Practice speaking and use proper grammar.

▼ Improve your writing habits.

▼ Don't say the same thing all the time—that is very boring!

▼ Read the newspaper—learn something new today.

▼ Stop blabbing, say it, just say it.

▼ Ask somebody if you want to know.

▼ Your thoughts count too!

▼ If you don't understand, say it. Get it straight!

▼ Never tell a lie!

Make them hear your speech!

Giving a speech makes most people nervous. Whenever I assign a speech I hear moans and groans from all of my students. They do their best and usually it is not so horrible, just not that great either.

A few years ago, I was grading speech after speech. The words sounded fake and phony and none of my students remembered to use eye contact, gestures, or a variety of speeds as they spoke. Some of the audience started to dose off, that is until Kenny stood up to make his speech.

> *Remember that first impressions really last! Get on the other person's good side from the start. Make each second count.*

His moves were smooth and confident. He greeted everyone and sat down on my desk with one foot on the desk and his arm wrapped around his knee. He began to speak and everyone noticed that his voice was quiet. They strained to listen and catch his eye.

I was in shock as I looked around the room and saw all eyes on Kenny. This guy was amazing and his speech was outstanding. He made sure that each person heard his message about smoking and cancer. You see this was very personal to him. His mom just died from lung cancer and she never smoked a cigarette in her life…he was the one who was smoking in the house and the second-hand smoke is what killed her.

Kenny admitted that he did not listen to advice to quit smoking. He thought that he could smoke as much as he wanted to because it was his life and he wanted to live as he chose. He shared his story and everyone paid attention because he was so passionate about the story.

Put your heart into your speech others will really hear you!

Your REPUTATION—It's all about YOU...

What other people say can help you or hurt you. Know this and protect your reputation. When you look for a job, you will need a list of teachers, neighbors, and associates that think highly of you. Before you give out this list, get their permission.

Want a job? Step #1 is writing your resume. Check out the appendix for some good examples. Feel free to copy down whatever you need.

Resumes list what you have done and what you can do for the company. Any honors? List them. Special skills? Know a foreign language? List that too.

Experiences make you more attractive...to employers!

Good student? Team member? Volunteer in the community?

These things add up to credibility. That stuff will make you look better than your competition.

Go to school? Did you graduate? That information counts!

Ask teachers and counselors about classes that may help you on a job.

Communication issues to think about...

Who cares about what they say?

What is the problem with the way most teens speak?

What is a good voice message?

What's that and when do you use it?
- ▼ PDA
- ▼ Cell phone
- ▼ 2-way
- ▼ Fax
- ▼ Email
- ▼ Snail mail

What is your problem, your words or their words?

First Impressions Last Forever!

During a recent school year, I was asked to find a student to write for a local newspaper. Most of my students were not interested in doing any extra writing and I became discouraged by their negative attitudes. After one of my classes, Shawna asked me for more some more details about this project. At that time, Shawna had no idea how important this opportunity would be for her.

She was asked to interview a local TV show host and then write a story about that person. Shawna and I had to visit the TV station, but had nothing to wear. I did not have much money to spend, but I went to Target and I found a black skirt suit for Shawna and it was less than $65.

When I gave her the suit, I don't think she loved it at first. Her face was happy, just not thrilled at the idea of wearing a business suit. I told her to trust me and she did. The next day, we both went to the TV station and met with a surprisingly down-to-earth celebrity. He was very impressed with her professional attire.

> *Get in the game! Everyone else is competition for the job you want. Know this: you must sell yourself, and outclass everybody else! A great image will set you apart from the crowd.*

As a matter of fact, he was so impressed that he asked her to be his guest on his next show! As she interviewed him about his climb to success, they also discussed her high school experiences. I joined in the conversation and mentioned that she is a great student looking for scholarships for college.

Why did I open my big mouth? I had a feeling that he could help her somehow. Well I was right! He served on the Board of Directors for a very elite university. He recommended her for a scholarship, gave her the contact names and numbers, and he made a few calls on her behalf—before we left the studio!

Shawna applied, was accepted and now she is doing very well in college. Her story ran in the paper and her interview aired on TV. Shawna has become the "poster girl" for looking professional.

Learn some new words!

Use past-tense power verbs on your resume to stand out on paper. Use a variety of career-related words in everyday conversations to stand out when you speak.

accountability	established	reported
accelerated	influenced	resume
achieved	generated	reviewed
adapted	gaudiness	revised
advised	freelance	saved
aerobic	enhanced	scheduled
applied	freelance	seminar
appointed	grammar	simplified
approved	interviewed	streamlined
appropriate	maintained	strengthened
assessed	monitored	succeeded
assisted	option	supervised
built	evaded	surpassed
brought	optimistic	supported
camouflage	posture	traditional
committed	prioritized	trained
communicated	promoted	treated
competed	proposed	transacted
computed	publicized	transferred
condiment	professional	translated
conducted	positive	uncovered
confirmed	protocol	utilized
demonstrated	recruited	verified
developed	reduced	won
distraction	reference	wrote
documented	recorded	
enhanced	reinforced	

He said, she said...

If you want to represent yourself properly, forget about:
- ▼ ghetto slang
- ▼ curse words
- ▼ big words you don't even understand

Don't be a phony! (body language)

People know when you tell a lie, so don't even try it.

You may say the right words, but your body tells on you.

Who are you afraid of? Stop looking down!

You talk too much? No one is listening to you. Get to the point.

No blah-blah-blah! Do not waste time with babbling on and on...

When someone is talking to you…

Bored? Too bad, pretend you are interested. You want something… so pay attention and learn something. Just chill, try not to fidget. Practice silence, this habit will serve you well!

Growing up is no joke! You're going to want what you want when you want it. Learn to give and then you will receive.

When somebody asks you something, be sure your *answers* are always serious. Don't waste time judging and giving your opinion. Unless you are calling the shots, no one cares what you think.

One more thing…learn how to give a firm, dry handshake!

The 411...on Habits worth forming...

▼ Check your sources. Make sure they really know what they are saying to you.

▼ Ain't too proud? Do not beg!

▼ When you make a deal, be sure that it works for you too.

▼ Do not waste your time or mine.

▼ Send handwritten "thank you" notes

▼ Leave clear telephone messages with your name, date, time, and your telephone number.

▼ Record a greeting on your phone, but don't play music and don't try to sound sexy

▼ Leave pagers, cell phones, and 2-ways "off" during class and at work

Where is Your Home-training?
Etiquette Matters

Eating Out?...Make A Good Impression

Eating at a restaurant is not the same as getting your grub on

What do I do with this napkin?

▼ Put it in your lap when you sit down

▼ Don't wipe off your whole face, show some class

▼ Touch your mouth gently

▼ Don't get the napkin all dirty

▼ Put napkin in your chair if you must leave during meal

▼ When you are finished, put napkin next to your plate

Where is your plate and which glasses are your glasses?

▼ B-M-W (left to right: bread—meal—water)

Placement of the utensils?

▼ Work from the outside to the inside with forks and knives .

▼ Place fork on left edge of plate and knife on right of plate during meal pauses

▼ When meal is finished, place both utensils together at 10 & 4 diagonal on plate with fork tongs down and knife with cutting edge towards you

Don't know what to order? Check out what everybody else orders. Make sure it is not sloppy— Spaghetti and ribs are too sloppy, order something else!

Bread/butter, condiments
- ▼ Tear a small piece of bread, butter it, eat it, pause, repeat
- ▼ Never cut a roll or butter the whole thing
- ▼ Pass salt and pepper to the person next to you
- ▼ Do not make too many requests
- ▼ Do not talk while eating
- ▼ Chew with mouth closed
- ▼ Take small bites
- ▼ Be polite, don't talk about religion, politics, or personal things like your dinner companion's weight
- ▼ Don't disrespect the waiters
- ▼ Whoever invites, should pay the bill

Traveling? Quick Tips for an Enjoyable Trip...

Airplanes

▼ Always call the 800 number to check last minute changes
▼ Get to the airport 2 hours before you leave
▼ Save time by checking in with the skycap (tip him $1.00 per bag)
▼ Take a snack in case the plane is late
▼ Ask an aisle seat for more room
▼ Take a magazine or a book
▼ Drink plenty of water

Packing Your bags

▼ Label with your name, address and phone
▼ Pack your bags with care
▼ Roll underwear and put socks inside shoes
▼ Don't try to pack you whole closet, take only a few things
▼ Wear your coat on the plane
▼ Stick with one basic dark color like African American or navy
▼ Bring a few accessories

Yes, you have to leave a tip!

▼ Doorman—give him a few bucks when you shake his hand
▼ Bellman—in your room, give him $1 for each bag
▼ Maid—leave a couple of bucks in room on the last day
▼ Waiter—leave 15% to 20% of the bill before tax

Tickets ...the Fun Stuff

▼ Museum—pay with cash on the day you go
▼ Concert or Sporting event—prepaid ticket

Rival Schools Meet

Sometimes, when you're away from home, there are choices to make and teens have to be allowed to make those choices. Act a fool or act like you have sense? It doesn't seem too hard to decide, but I am not a teenager.

A few years back, two groups of students shared the same room at a luncheon. There was plenty of food, but only one school could get in line at a time. They played great music, for a white DJ, he was really good. But the dance floor was not that big, so some people bumped into each other. The two schools were from rival sides of the city, each thinking they were the toughest. Finally, both sets of students were getting ready to graduate.

The adults in this picture had a quick conference to compare notes and a plan of action should anything jump off. The music started playing and the butts started to shake. The guys were dancing around one girl and the arms were flying back and forth…to the beat.

One teacher parted the crowd and found a shock: a senior boy from one school was showing a teacher from the other school how to dance. Everyone was cheering, not screaming for a fight. As the afternoon went on, the two schools danced, chanted, ate lunch, and shared congratulations.

Focus on the other person and learn something!

The surprise for the teachers was that a senior class from a South Side high school could interact and serve as role-models for an 8th grade class from the West Side. These kids set a new standard for scheduling events for schools to share a room. The teachers gave out special awards at both graduation ceremonies, not from their schools, but from the other schools for being so mannerable.

That event also made the 6 o'clock news. These schools had never been friendly to each other and the rest of the city needed to hear about this group of kids with such nice manners.

Staying in touch the right way...

Making phone calls:
- ▼ Say hello, give your full name, and ask if the person is available.

Answering the phone:
- ▼ Say, "Good morning, this is Robin Collymore, how may I help you?" Be polite if you screen calls, say "May I tell him/her who is calling?"

Leaving messages:
- ▼ Leave your full name, phone number, and reason for the call.

Speakerphones:
- ▼ Don't even try this unless you have permission!

FAX:
- ▼ Send a cover sheet listing the total number of pages to follow.

Email:
- ▼ For business, be polite and get to the point.
- ▼ With your friends, don't send anything impolite...you know what I mean!

Cell phones:
- ▼ These are not for long conversations. Use for emergencies and checking in with your people. Leave cell phones on vibrate or "off" when you go to class, church or meetings.

Letters:
- ▼ Thank you notes—handwritten and specific
- ▼ Titles—Mr/Mrs/Ms; Sir/Madame
- ▼ Address the envelope—company, dept, name, address
- ▼ Invitations—include stamped r.s.v.p.

Where Are Your Manners? ...
Test Your Knowledge Now...

▼ It is fun to flirt and it's ok to flirt anywhere at anytime?
True or False?

▼ At a restaurant with several other people, you should always start to eat your food when...

▼ Girls should hold the door for guys.
Why?

▼ You should play games like tennis and golf just to show off your new shoes.
True or False

Explain your answer

▼ At the dinner table, where is your butter dish?

▼ Can you draw a picture of a formal setting?

▼ Gangsta Rap, and Hip-Hop are cool, but what are Jazz, Gospel, and The Blues?

Fit in or get out

At the end of four years of high school, Michael just knew that no one could touch him. He'd passed every single class, turned in all of his projects, collected signatures from each teacher and he was in the auditorium at graduation rehearsal. Life was good, real good for Michael and he was ready to celebrate, laugh, joke, and have some fun.

He grew bored of the directions being barked out by Mrs. Stillman, the coordinator. This woman needed to lose weight, get some new clothes and wear some makeup. She was not a bad person, but she kept talking about boring stuff like being polite, listening to directions, and following her lead. Michael was bored and he could not take it anymore.

Out of his mouth came insults, one after another. He screamed, he laughed, he mocked her words. He made everyone around him turn and stare at him because he was so very rude. Mrs. Stillman just looked blankly in his direction, blurted out a threat and continued to give directions. Michael told her to get out and then he would be quiet.

> *When you want a job, a scholarship, a better grade, or just some respect, act like you deserve it. BEHAVE!*

Mrs. Stillman did just that, she walked out. The rehearsal continued without Michael's mouth and everyone enjoyed the rest of the day. Mrs. Stillman went to the ladies' room to relax and refocus. The principal saw Mrs. Stillman in the ladies' room and asked why she was crying. "I am so very embarrassed that these African American children have no respect for this ceremony. I am tired of working to reach out to them and then one kid ruins everything by cracking jokes!"

The principal called Michael's parents and they came up to the school. They assumed that something was wrong, and they were right. The principal handed them Michael's diploma and they also had to take Michael home from school and promise not to show up at the graduation!

The pitiful part came when Michael's grandparents, cousins, aunts, and uncles got off the train from Memphis. Since there was no graduation ceremony, there were no graduation gifts for Michael!

Never, ever allow bad behavior to ruin your chance to benefit from a great situation. Good manners will never get you into trouble. Bad manners can cost you more than you know!

For all the Haters ... We know who you are!
Acting out gets you nowhere! When you are:

Aggressive

Rude

Hostile

Prejudiced

Ignorant

Bored

Know the GAME!

Show your skills, but know the rules. Adults in business play lots of games. Check your ego at the door and learn some new skills. You just might close the deal on some big business one day!

> *Pull yourself together. Look good, but not like a lame with ghetto-fab gear on and gym shoes that cost too much.*

Here's something to think about....

Basketball shoes can make you or break you?

If you answered YES, please keep reading...

It's not about who wins the game. Style and manners count more than points. These are mind games, be cool, and never let them see you sweat!

Be a player...just remember to handle your business!

Chess

- ▼ Show thoughtful planning skills
- ▼ One-on-one competition
- ▼ Use your brain
- ▼ For rules: United States Chess Federation

Golf

- ▼ Shows your true character
- ▼ Chance to get to know a person
- ▼ For rules: Multi-Cultural Golf Association of America (WWW.MGAA.COM)

Tennis

- ▼ Shows your flexibility
- ▼ Play on a team or as a single
- ▼ For rules: United States Tennis Association

Racquetball

- ▼ Got strength, prove it
- ▼ Get a great workout
- ▼ For rules: United States Racquetball Association

The 411 on Going Out and Handling your Business Properly!

▼ Reach out and shake hands firmly.

▼ Sit when told to sit at the office, interview, dinner

▼ Listen, learn, don't interrupt with silly remarks

▼ Introductions, name of highest ranking person first

▼ Want to get along? Let people talk about themselves!

▼ Wear nametags on the right shoulder because the eye follows the handshake to the right shoulder

Going to College?
Apply For All Scholarships!

Do your best to get a scholarship!

Get good grades

▼ Do all of your work
▼ Talk with your teachers

Do your community service

▼ Meet new people
▼ Get job experience

Write letters to be changed for each scholarship

▼ Why I want to attend this college/university…
▼ My biggest challenge is…
▼ I am the best for this scholarship because…
▼ My strengths and weaknesses are…

Work with your counselors because...

▼ They know the rules and deadlines
▼ They know businesses with money for young people
▼ They know how to help you to succeed

Get summer jobs

▼ Make some money
▼ Handle your own money
▼ Learn to work with others

Help out

▼ Check out a job
▼ Meet people with power

Visit many colleges

▼ Figure out what you love or hate
▼ Talk to real college students for the real deal

The A-Student Who Did Not Know How to Study

Going to college is a very serious time in a teenager's life. No one knows everything, but Ruthie thought she knew it all! She knew what to wear, how to do her hair, and most of all what parties to attend. When it came to school and her studies, Ruthie figured she could do it later. Somehow setting aside time to study was not at the top of her list.

> *College life is full of decisions. Some decisions are much easier than others. Other decisions are simple and should be very clear. Ruthie thought that she could go to class, take a few notes and then forget about hitting her books until the next class.*

Each morning she did the same things. She went to breakfast late and never ate any fruit, or cereal, she just ate donuts. She went to class at the last minute and missed the opening of most of the lectures. She sat in the back, yawned and sometimes went to sleep during class. If she had been to a great party the night before, many days she would cut class just to sleep longer.

In the afternoons when her friends were studying, Ruthie was on the phone or at the mall. She spent her entire student loan check on outfits for the sorority and fraternity parties on campus. Every week she had to get a manicure, pedicure, eyebrow wax, and deep conditioning treatment at the local spa. The other girls just did their own hair, nails and grooming, but Ruthie was very spoiled and had her own standards to maintain.

In the evenings she watched TV and went out to eat, every college town has great pizza and that was her favorite. She did not make the time to study and she laughed at her friends who appeared weary after a long night of research at the library. Ruthie thought that college was easy and she never understood why everyone else had to spend so much time reading, writing, meeting with professors, and looking up information at the library.

When the time came for the final exams, Ruthie was confident that she was prepared. Each class was easier than the first and Ruthie was happy to end her first semester as a college student. She finished all of her tests, packed her bags and went home for a 30-day winter vacation.

About a week later, a package arrived for Ruthie's parents. Since she thought she knew what was inside the package, she begged her mom to open it up quickly. She said to her mom, "How many A's and how many B's?" Her mom's face was very stiff and her left eyebrow went up as she said, "You have wasted your time and my money. Your grades are terrible and you have been placed on academic probation!"

Ruthie was crushed. She cried for 2 whole days. Her mom and dad decided to give her some advice. "Go to see your academic advisor and ask for some help," they said. When she got back to her campus, Ruthie remembered that advice. After a long conversation, the counselor smiled and said, "Ruthie you are like many other A students. You did not learn to study in high school. Good grades have always been easy for you. C students learned to study much better than A students because C students struggled to get their grades. Just because you made the high honor roll, National Honor Society, and had your name listed in Who's Who does not mean you know how to study! You must take time to go over your books and notes after every class. Read and review, read ahead and write out some questions. Get an appointment with each teacher and make sure they know that you want to succeed!"

Ruthie took that advice and made sure that academics were her first priority. She did graduate on time, but she missed a few trips to the mall and quite a few manicures! Now she advises other college students not to make no mistakes!

Planning your College Schedule

Your Classes

▼ Schedule your classes the way you want them

▼ That way you can go to class when you want to go!

▼ For example, no classes before 10am with Fridays FREE:
Math 101 MW 10a-12p
Eng 102 TuTh 2p-330p
Psych 160 MW 2p-330p
Pol Sci 100 Tu 7p-10p
Bio 100 TuTh 12p-1p

Your Teachers

▼ Check with older students in your major to get references

▼ Look at all of the times available before choosing your schedule

▼ Ask for help from your counselor before choosing a teacher, section, or time

Your Study Partners

▼ Find someone different, from a different culture/race/country/state/background to be your study partner

▼ They will see things from a different viewpoint and you will learn from them

▼ It is better to study by yourself AND with a buddy to share and compare

Study Guidelines

Before your classes:
- ▼ Read the assigned chapters in your books
- ▼ Take notes
- ▼ Write questions
- ▼ Think about what you will learn in class

During your classes:
- ▼ Take really good notes
- ▼ Everything on your tests is not always in your books
- ▼ Ask questions

After your classes:
- ▼ Review your notes
- ▼ Re-read the chapters
- ▼ Write questions and answers

During the business hours of 9am-5pm (40 hrs/week)

▼ Your classes should not take more than 18 hours each week
▼ Study during the other 22 hours
▼ Remain on schedule and you will not fall behind or miss out on any fun!

Work with your teachers and counselors:

▼ Make appointments to talk with them during office hours
▼ Stay after class to ask a question
▼ Join career-related clubs
▼ Volunteer to gain job experience
▼ Join a sorority or fraternity to meet network with other professionals
▼ Do temporary work
▼ Sign up for an internship in your field
▼ Get to know the alumni association members and ask them for help

Some Students Have it ALL

Darnell wanted to be outstanding. He was not a sports superstar. He did not have a lot of girlfriends. He did not drive a fabulous car. He did not have a lot of money. He was smart, and he had a plan. From the first day at school, he knew that he could get into trouble if he tried to be a know-it-all. He was careful about letting his classmates know about his intelligence.

He was not afraid, but Darnell was street smart, not just book smart. He worked on his own and in groups. He shared his ideas, but did not push them on anyone. Soon, his teachers began to praise him and his classmates looked up to him.

> *No one made fun of him and no one ever called him names. Everyone, especially the roughest kids in the school really liked Darnell because he never made anyone else feel dumb or stupid.*

Darnell began to think about college during his sophomore year in high school. He spent the summer before his junior year at a college campus. During that summer, he met students from other cities and they all lived in the dorms. They had to get up and get to class on time. They had to wash their own clothes. They had to study before and after each class and they had to take tests.

This experience was good for Darnell. He learned at an early age how to study, how to get ahead, and how to be successful in college. This experience gave Darnell focus. He found it very easy to make decisions about going out or staying in to study. He missed quite a few parties because he was busy applying for scholarships. He joined the debate team and traveled to visit many college campuses.

Darnell planned to be successful in college and prepared for that time while he was still in high school. He was not perfect, Darnell actually got into trouble from time to time for being late to class or cutting class. He always explained what was going on to his teachers, and he learned to get permission to miss class instead of just cutting the class. He was not afraid to admit that he was afraid of failure and never wanted to end up like so many others in his family.

Today, Darnell is in college on a full-ride academic scholarship. He gets homesick and spends a lot of time sending emails to friends at other campuses. Darnell is a Business major and plans to become the Chief Executive Officer of a major corporation after he earns his Masters degree in Business Administration. Based on his successes, Darnell is on the right path because he began his plan at an early age.

Look EVERYWHERE for scholarships!

Businesses
- ▼ Your parents' companies
- ▼ Parents' clubs
- ▼ Neighborhood stores
- ▼ Car dealers
- ▼ Grocery stores
- ▼ Companies in your city
- ▼ Corporations in your state
- ▼ Franchised businesses/Fast-food restaurants

Education/Government Agencies
- ▼ Public schools in your city/town
- ▼ Junior Colleges
- ▼ Universities
- ▼ City/State/Federal offices

Non-Profit Groups
- ▼ Churches
- ▼ Youth organizations
- ▼ Corporation non-profit departments
- ▼ Hospitals

Media Outlets
- ▼ Radio stations
- ▼ TV stations
- ▼ Magazines
- ▼ Newspapers
- ▼ Internet websites
- ▼ Publishers
- ▼ Advertising agencies

Your Favorite Businesses/Companies

▼ Banks
▼ Professional Sports teams & leagues
▼ Clothing stores
▼ Record companies
▼ Athletic shoe companies
▼ Underwear manufacturers
▼ Cosmetic companies
▼ Computer companies
▼ School supply companies

Vital Words: Be a Professional

▼ Be *polite* at all times! It will not hurt! Our manners and our concern for others show our own dignity. Listen to others. Say please and thank you. Share eye contact or a smile. Treat your friends, family and teachers with the same respect you want from them.

▼ Be *realistic* about work-related situations! Work like a team-mate to get the job done without stress. Nothing is ever perfect and no one has all of the answers. Usually others are not trying to cause you any personal harm.

▼ Be *optimistic* and have a good attitude! It will give you energy, no kidding! See the positive not the negative side of everything. Find a solution to a problem; don't let it get bigger. If you always complain, you will be considered petty, insecure, untrustworthy and immature.

▼ Be *flexible* with your skills and activities. You need to set yourself apart from everyone else when you want a promotion. Try to do more than is expected and the ability to do that job well will give you a competitive edge. Your boss will take note and remember the little things that you do that make his/her job much easier. This flexibility is required of all employees planning to move up the corporate ladder.

▼ Be more *effective* at everything that you do. Putting in a bit more effort will make the difference between doing a job and doing it well! Add more effort whenever you do anything. See the process through to completion. Think through any potential problems and solve them before they occur.

▼ Be *stronger* by becoming physically fit. Healthy people are less likely to take days off for sickness. They exude the confidence and ability to pay attention to details. Fit individuals emanate qualities of strength, confidence and stamina.

▼ Be *sure* to know that your talent is needed to get the job done. Try becoming a part of a company that provides some service or product. Always remember that you are important. Enjoy your job and provide your services with confidence and with a smile. Remember that others are waiting to take your place.

▼ Be more *independent* so that others can depend on you. Being able to work on a team is vital in any job. However, never forget that your work must be done independently and with as little supervision as possible. Try to resolve your own problems and present your supervisor with the problem *and* your solution for permission to complete the task more effectively. Making the situation easier for your boss will make you more valuable.

▼ Be *organized!* Be neat in appearance, have a neat, clutter-free workstation. The image that you present from head to toe, with your written projects, in your verbal communication, and your desk, cubicle or office, give an overall impression of your strengths. Even if you are not strong in every area, being organized will distract others from your weaknesses.

▼ Be *non-confrontational* at all times. Maintain your cool when disappointed, angry, scared, or tired. "Never let them see you sweat!" Handle difficult challenges with pride and dignity. Be like water, strong, yet supple, consistent, but yielding.

▼ Be *approachable.* Reach out to people, listen to their words and pay attention to their actions. Respond the right way and be certain that you are giving your best effort in all situations. Form friendly bonds, but do not get too personal. Know how to listen without telling intimate details about you. Be friendly, but with a professional distance.

▼ Be *loyal* to your company, your manager, and most of all, to your team. Make others shine and you too, will shine. Make the job easy for your boss and you will be rewarded in the future. Think like a manager and do your best to make his/her job easier.

The 411 on Completing Your College & Scholarship Application

Type information
- ▼ Save on a diskette
- ▼ Write generic letters to be personalized as needed

Keep a file
- ▼ Make copies for future reference
- ▼ Know what you sent, to whom, and specific dates

Be very neat
- ▼ Avoid mistakes with spell check
- ▼ Have someone else look it over
- ▼ Never get document dirty or wet

Do everything on time
- ▼ Meet deadlines
- ▼ Call for next steps

Follow-up
- ▼ Call to check status
- ▼ Ask questions
- ▼ Know when you have made it or missed out

Ask for help from decision-makers
- ▼ Make appointment for a face-to-face meeting
- ▼ Make a great impression

Focus on your leadership
- ▼ Regardless of activity, show your contributions
- ▼ List all of your titles

The Right Stuff
Resumes, Cover Letters, Job Applications

What do they want?

Teachers, Professors, Supervisors, Managers, Bosses—they all want something:

Smart people who learn information well
- ▼ Computer programming
- ▼ Word-processing
- ▼ Teaching
- ▼ Cooking
- ▼ Purchasing
- ▼ Repairing
- ▼ Analyzing
- ▼ Counseling

Nice people who get along with others well
- ▼ Leading
- ▼ Producing
- ▼ Reporting
- ▼ Constructing
- ▼ Organizing
- ▼ Teaching
- ▼ Encouraging

Mature people who know themselves well
- ▼ Courage
- ▼ Concern
- ▼ Stability
- ▼ Integrity
- ▼ Promptness
- ▼ Patience

Follow these hints to write a great resume...

Format
- ▼ List your skills first
- ▼ Tell what you can do for them
- ▼ Make it short and sweet
- ▼ Look at the next page for more...

Focus
- ▼ Make them want you! (Highlight the right skills for each job)
- ▼ Brag a little! (Recognized as top salesperson during 2002)
- ▼ Use numbers (Saved 45% of previous expenses)

Information
- ▼ Use the right words
- ▼ Check out the want ads for new ideas
- ▼ No personal information about age, race or health
- ▼ Do not lie

References
- ▼ Have at least 1 professional, 1 personal, and 1 academic reference
- ▼ Only give references when they ask for it

Resume appearance
- ▼ Must be as perfect
- ▼ No typos or spelling errors
- ▼ Neat and clean

Resumes Do Matter!!—Sometimes Being Too Cool Is Not Cool At All

The Speech teacher talked too much and lectured too much and demanded too much out of Erika. She hated this class because Mrs. Smithers spoke her mind and knew just what Erika was thinking at all times. If Erika rolled her eyes at a comment, Mrs. Smithers walked right over to her just to be sure that Erika understood the assignment. Mrs. Smithers always smiled and complimented Erika on her answers and told her to try again when her answers were incomplete.

Erika had to admit that Mrs. Smithers knew her very well, but that is why she hated this teacher so much. Every assignment had to be turned in. All of the students had to work together to make sure the projects were completed and the whole team understood the process. The worst part was when Mrs. Smithers asked the students to plan their ideal class project. Erika said she wanted to be the project leader and Mrs. Smithers agreed that she should be the leader. Erika just wanted to throw up, but she went to class every day just to pick on Mrs. Smithers.

The other students in the class were not as supportive of Erika as the teacher. They called her stupid for acting that way. They told her that this was their favorite class because they were really learning how to work as a team and how to get ready for the workforce. Erika tried to block everything good about that class. She asked to go to the bathroom just before her resume was due. She stayed in the bathroom because she wanted to stall around and miss most of the class and miss giving her speech and presented her resume. Mrs. Smithers was waiting for Erika after class. Erika walked into the room very slowly and tried not to look at her teacher.

> *Know the real deal. When you have a plan, sometimes others have the final say over what will be. Here is the inside scoop: people with power will judge you. This may be the cops, a teacher, or a manager.*

"Did you do your resume?" said Mrs. Smithers.

"Yep, here it is," said Erika.

"This resume is not at all what we discussed in class. Everyone else in your group agreed on a format, but you just have a list of jobs without any support. I wish that you had followed the format."

"Who cares?" said Erika. "This is my resume, I can do it any way that I want to do it. I don't care about anybody's format. This looks good to me. Who cares what you think!"

"Very well, Erika, turn it in and I will grade it," said Mrs. Smithers, "have a nice afternoon and I will see you tomorrow."

The next day, Mrs. Smithers had a special guest speaker visit the class. Mr. Anders was the owner of a local business and he was there to hire students for summer jobs. The resume assignment was part of a plan to prepare students to join the workforce and Mrs. Smithers submitted the resumes to Mr. Anders to help her class find jobs.

Everyone was hired except for Erika. Mr. Anders thought that her sloppy resume indicated that she would be a problem at the work site. He felt since she was too cool to do her homework, she would not fit into his company. She missed the chance to earn money and a college scholarship. Being cool like Erika is never cool in the long run.

Fill in the blanks for a rough draft of your own resume

HEADING *(don't type each word)*

Name_____

Address, city, state, and zip code_____

Telephone _____

Email_____

OBJECTIVE (you can type all of these words)

To use my _____ skills to enhance

_____ at a _____ company.

QUALIFICATIONS
(List computer skills, software skills, and specialized training)

_____

_____

_____

WORK EXPERIENCE
Start date—End date _____-_____

Job Title, Name of company, city, state_____

_____

Use powerful verbs to start each line
(See examples of this section on next page)

EDUCATION

Degree or diploma earned and date received _____

_____

Name of school, college or university, city, and state _____

_____

AWARDS/ASSOCIATIONS

Title of award, organization and date of award _____

Name of organizations _____

Offices held_____

REFERENCES

Available upon request

Examples of Work Experience...

The following examples will show you how to show potential employers that your work experience has given you valuable skills. Notice the words in **bold.** Use percentages and numbers. Show your accomplishments.

Sales Clerk

▼ **Initiated** customer service techniques as representative of large retail outlet

▼ **Requested** follow-up and additional documentation as needed to improve quality of service

▼ **Collaborated** with members of departmental team to execute standards and policies prioritized by management

▼ **Developed** streamlined procedures for enhancements of daily waste management

▼ **Increased** profits of operation by 20% with coordination of volunteer activities

▼ **Saved** $10,000 from annual expenditures with negotiations with domestic and international vendors

▼ **Enacted** team and department competition to build confidence, interdependence and recreation into after-work hours

Coach

▼ **Demonstrated** proper techniques for 30 youth athletes

▼ **Interacted** with 50% of clientele

▼ **Organized** and implemented recreational activities

▼ **Evaluated** levels of advancement for specialized reports

▼ **Documented** attendance and participation as legally required

Tutor
- ▼ **Implemented** educational support initiative of major non-profit organization

- ▼ **Interacted** with school-aged students in need of one-to-one tutorial services

- ▼ **Planned, prepared and presented** nourishing meals for 75 children on a daily basis

- ▼ **Evaluated and recommended** improvements to insure future profitability

Crew Member
- ▼ **Prepared** meals to meet industry standards for taste, appearance, and texture

- ▼ **Negotiated** with customers to increase sales by 35%

- ▼ **Documented** 55% of inter-office correspondence

- ▼ **Researched** background of applicants prior to employment

- ▼ **Referred** 25% of all new hires for additional training incentive programs

Start with past-tense power verbs—sometimes that is all they read anyway!

Cover Letters

Why write a cover letter?
▼ Make them want to meet you!
▼ Stand out from the crowd
▼ Be more **personal**

Great cover letters have:
▼ Information about the **JOB**!
▼ Your **QUALIFICATIONS** for this job
▼ Request an **INTERVIEW**!

Check out this example:

Your address
City, State, Zip code
Date

His/her name
Title
Company
Address
City, State, Zip

Dear _____:

(paragraph #1 mention the job!)
I am responding to your ad in the (newspaper, Internet, TV, radio, etc.) for the position of _____.

(paragraph #2 point out your qualifications!)
I have enclosed my resume. You will notice that I am qualified for this position based on my experience as _____.

(paragraph #3 ask for an interview!)
I want to schedule an interview as soon as possible. You can call me at (_____) or email me at _____@_____.com. On _____, I will follow up with you with a telephone call.

Thank you for your consideration,

Your name

The Job Application

- ▼ Typed or handwritten

- ▼ Practice filling out several applications

- ▼ Be sure it is complete

- ▼ Use pen, not pencil

- ▼ Mail or hand deliver it

- ▼ Be very neat

- ▼ Think about answers before writing

- ▼ Use N/A, don't leave any blank sections

- ▼ Attach your resume if possible

The 411 on Promoting Yourself as THE Best!

Believe you can FLY!
- ▼ Write a short commercial about yourself
- ▼ Think of questions and answers

Act like you know something!
- ▼ Check out the job first
- ▼ Speak their language
- ▼ Get there 10 minutes early
- ▼ Check out everyone in the office
- ▼ Know that hey are watching you too

Look like you mean business!
- ▼ Clothes straight?
- ▼ Stand still!
- ▼ Look cool!

Lights, Camera, Action
Pull It All Together For Your Interview

Interview Questions

1. Why are you the best person for this job?

2. How do you handle stressful changes and challenges?

3. Why should I hire you?

4. How much money are you worth?

5. Tell me what you know about our company.

6. What are your weaknesses?

7. What is your idea of a typical day at work?

8. Describe your work ethic.

9. What would others say about you and your skills?

10. Why do you want to work here?

Looking for a job? Going to college? Need a scholarship?

Keep on reading...

▼ Check them out…
▼ Do they have what you want?
▼ What do they want you to do?
▼ Will you fit in?
▼ How will you get there on time every day?
▼ What about the benefits?
▼ When will you get a raise?

Do it right...

▼ Sit when invited to do so
▼ Shake hands
▼ Look interviewer in the eye
▼ Give short answers, but answer the questions

Be ready for the question anywhere, anytime...

▼ At a game: know the rules
▼ Somebody's house: know your manners
▼ Party: know how to work the room
▼ Restaurant: know how to order

Successful Interviews—Putting it all together, preparation, looks, effort

Alicia was not the one to give advice. She had her own look and never shared her secrets with anyone. She always seemed prepared to handle just about anything that came her way. She liked men, not boys and made no excuse for her flirty ways with the Security staff and her favorite Football coach. She looked good and knew what to do to get attention.

During her senior year in high school, she had a chance to interview for a job at a local radio station. She wrote out a resume and followed the guidelines in a booklet from her counselor's office. She bought a short skirt suit and a low cut blouse. Her black high heels made the outfit just right and she felt that she was ready for her interview.

During a classroom discussion, Alicia learned that looking really sexy may not be the best look for an interview. She said, "I need to show them what I am working with and I know that I will get any job I want!" The teacher smiled and added, "Alicia, you are supposed to encourage the interviewer to listen to you and learn about your qualifications, not look you up and down and make a decision."

After class, Alicia stayed to have a longer conversation. She learned that interview suits are basic and usually dark with a blouse or shirt. The jewelry is limited to a watch and small earrings for ladies. This bleak outfit is more of a uniform and wearing this uniform gives the interviewer the signal that this person knows what to do and what is appropriate.

> *The purpose of wearing the interview uniform is to make sure that the other person concentrates on the applicant's qualifications.*

Alicia asked some very important questions and decided to reconsider her choice of interview suits. The next day was her big interview. She wore a longer skirt and buttoned her blouse up. She replaced her big hoop earrings with small studs and decided not to have the tri-colored rainbows painted on her nails as she normal did.

After the interview, Alicia was proud of herself. She received three compliments about her professional attire and manners. The next day she got a call. She got the job! Next she went shopping for more business clothes!

The real deal: The interview, the meeting, the speech...

- ▼ Know something? Prove it!
- ▼ How can you help them?
- ▼ This is only business
- ▼ Ask your own questions
- ▼ If they disrespect you, it's over!
- ▼ Find a good fit
- ▼ How do they make money?

After the interview...Thank you notes

- ▼ Hand written notes are best
- ▼ Tell them what you learned in the interview
- ▼ Get to the point
- ▼ Send it out the next day

Follow up

- ▼ Pick up the phone

Next steps...

- ▼ Get ready for the next interviews

What is a network?

Your network is all of the people that **you know** and **the people** that **they know** too!

Family network:
- ▼ parents
- ▼ uncles
- ▼ in-laws
- ▼ neighbors
- ▼ dentists
- ▼ aunts
- ▼ cousins
- ▼ friends
- ▼ doctors
- ▼ nurses

School network:
- ▼ teachers
- ▼ counselors
- ▼ club sponsors
- ▼ club members
- ▼ parents' former classmates
- ▼ church-members
- ▼ ministers

Job Network:
- ▼ supervisor
- ▼ boss
- ▼ co-workers
- ▼ teammates
- ▼ coaches
- ▼ local business people

Know someone with the job you want? Get real close; cause one day you will need them!

This is your **network of contacts.** Learn from this network. Ask them for advice. Trust their judgments. Do what they say. Tell them what you want to do with your life.

Want a job...Get ready to work!

Get out of the house!
- ▼ Talk to friends and family
- ▼ Call your teachers and counselors
- ▼ Make lists of everyone and anyone and call them too

Look in the mirror!
- ▼ Know your strengths and weaknesses
- ▼ Remember successes and failures

Write a short commercial about you
- ▼ Know what you can and will do
- ▼ Practice your speech

Write a resume
- ▼ Make several copies
- ▼ Keep a copy with you

Keep your mind open
- ▼ Go for your dream, but get a job
- ▼ You never know who can help

Have a free makeover
- ▼ Go to the mall
- ▼ Ask the barber/stylist for new ideas

Go into a large business office building, look around, listen and take notes

Get a job, any job!

Work at home
- ▼ Baby-sit
- ▼ Type
- ▼ Run errands
- ▼ Walk dogs
- ▼ Mow lawns
- ▼ Clean up

Get some experience
- ▼ Don't reject anything
- ▼ Volunteer

Look good all the time
- ▼ Your hair is everything
- ▼ Exercise and eat right
- ▼ Help somebody
- ▼ Wash your clothes
- ▼ Shine your shoes

Talk to everyone
- ▼ Who do you know who can help you?
- ▼ Where can you meet new people to help you?
- ▼ Have you ever helped anyone else?
- ▼ Write, call, email, and fax!

Get ready for rejection
- ▼ You won't always win!
- ▼ Do not give up
- ▼ Ask for help
- ▼ Apply again and again
- ▼ Write and complain if necessary

The 411 on Outshining the competition

▼ Be *polite* at all times! Show your home training!

▼ Be for real! Nobody is perfect, deal with it!

▼ Get a better attitude! Quit complaining all the time. It just brings everybody down

▼ Don't sweat the small stuff!

▼ Get better! Just get better!

▼ Get buffed!

▼ Work alone or work together, just work it right!

▼ Go with the flow! Get yourself organized!

▼ Be very clean! Enough said…

▼ Be friendly!

▼ Stand up for something important!

▼ Have some pride!

Conclusion

Most of us are feel very strongly about something important. I am focused on making sure that young people have the options in life to make choices to live happy and healthy lives. This choice requires preparation, education and opportunity. My hope is that my students and my readers are educated and prepared for all opportunities!

It is my dream that *No Mistakes—The African American Teen Guide for Growing Up Strong* will give you the necessary details about maintaining a job and growing in your career.

Stay blessed

Robin Henry

About the Author—
Fact Sheet

▼ Mom to my son: Grayson Mitchell (successful scholar, athlete & my greatest joy)

▼ Managing Editor: NOIRWoman Newspaper

▼ Newspaper Columnist: "Style" *(Waukegan People's Voice)*

▼ "Details Count" *(Houston Informer)*

▼ Radio Show Host: "Are you Ready to Work" (WLTH-AM)

▼ TV Show Host: "CABJ-TV" (CAN Television Chicago)

▼ Educator: Curr Coord/ H.S. English Teacher/ Dept Chair (Chgo Public Schools)

▼ Media Consultant: (Advertising agencies and Public Relations firms)

▼ Member: Alpha Kappa Alpha Sorority, Inc. (Theta Omega Chapter)

▼ Certified Professional Development Trainer (Professional Woman's Network)

▼ Resume Consultant

▼ Self-proclaimed expert on travel, shopping, eating, and hair!

An acronym for my names and my diverse career, RCMedia symbolizes the power of working with many resources to achieve a goal. I have diverse professional experiences, unique talents and insights; and I have the goal of providing valuable information so that others can attain those professional skills required to:

▼ Exude confidence

▼ Secure employment opportunities

▼ Positively influence decision-makers

▼ Reinvent one's self in times of unintentional unemployment

Notes

ORDER FORM

WWW.AMBERBOOKS.COM
African-American Self Help and Celebrity Bios

Fax Orders: 480-283-0991   Postal Orders: Send Checks & Money Orders to:
Telephone Orders: 480-460-1660   Amber Books Publishing
Online Orders: E-mail: Amberbks@aol.com   1334 E. Chandler Blvd., Suite 5-D67
                                         Phoenix, AZ 85048

_____*No Mistakes: The African-American Teen Guide to Growing Up Strong*
_____*The African-American Teenagers Guide to Personal Growth, Health, Safety, Sex and Survival*
_____*Born Beautiful: The African-American Teenagers Complete Beauty Guide*
_____*Divas of the New Millenium*
_____*Is Modeling for You?*
_____*Fighting for Your Life*
_____*Your Body's Calling Me: The Life & Times of "Robert" R. Kelly*
_____*Ready to Die: Notorious B.I.G.*
_____*Beautiful Black Hair: A Step-by-Step Instructional Guide*
_____*Aaliyah—An R&B Princess in Words and Pictures*
_____*Christina Aguilera: A Star is Born*
_____*You Forgot About Dre: Dr. Dre & Eminem*
_____*The African-American Job Seeker's Guide to Successful Employment*
_____ *How to Play the Sports Recruiting Game*
_____*Suge Knight: The Rise, Fall, and Rise of Death Row Records*
_____*50 Cent: No Holds Barred*
_____*Jay-Z…and the Roc-A-Fella Dynasty*
_____*Tupac Shakur—(2-Pac) In The Studio*
_____*The African-American Music Instruction Guide for Piano*

Name:_____
Company Name:_____
Address:_____
City:_____ State:_____ Zip:_____
Telephone: (_____) _____ E-mail:_____

For Bulk Rates Call: **480-460-1660**   # ORDER NOW

No Mistakes	$14.95	☐ Check ☐ Money Order ☐ Cashiers Check
Teenagers Guide	$19.95	☐ Credit Card: ☐ MC ☐ Visa ☐ Amex ☐
Born Beautiful	$14.95	Discover
Divas of the New Millenium	$16.95	
Is Modeling for You?	$14.95	CC#_____
Fighting for Your Life	$14.95	
R Kelly	$16.95	Expiration Date:_____
Notorius BIG	$16.95	
Beautiful Black Hair	$16.95	**Payable to:** Amber Books
Aaliyah	$10.95	1334 E. Chandler Blvd., Suite 5-D67
Christina Aguilera	$12.95	Phoenix, AZ 85048
You Forgot About Dre	$10.95	
Job Seeker's Guide	$14.95	**Shipping:** $5.00 per book. Allow 7 days
Sports Recruiting	$12.95	for delivery.
Suge Knight	$21.95	**Sales Tax:** Add 7.05% to books shipped to
50 Cent	$16.95	Arizona addresses.
Jay-Z	$16.95	**Total enclosed: $**_____
Tupac Shakur	$16.95	
Piano Instruction Guide	$14.95	